GW00771417

Miracle Man Handbook

A Christian guide to a good life

Linda Schubert

Other books by Linda Schubert

Miracle Hour
True Confessions
Precious Power
Miracle Moments
The Healing Power of a Father's Blessing
Five Minute Miracles
Rich in Mercy
Miracle Woman Handbook

First printing November 2006

Cover design by
Andre Adams
www.andreadams.com
email andreadams1974@yahoo.com

All scripture quotations are from the
New International Version of the Bible

Linda Schubert
Miracles of the Heart Ministries
PO Box 4034
Santa Clara CA 95056
Phone (408) 734-8663
fax (408) 734-8661
email linda@linda-schubert.com

Miracle Man Handbook
A Christian guide to a good life

Table of Contents

I pray for you "... asking God to fill you with the knowledge of His will through all spiritual wisdom and understanding...in order that you might live a life worthy of the Lord and please Him in every way; bearing fruit in every good work, growing in the knowledge of God, being strengthened with all power according to his glorious might so that you may have great endurance and patience, and joyfully giving thanks to the Father, who has qualified you to share in the inheritance of the saints in the kingdom of light" (Col 1:9-12).

Miracle Man Handbook
A Christian guide to a good life

Introduction

"I keep asking that the God of our Lord Jesus Christ, the glorious Father, may give you the Spirit of wisdom and revelation, so that you may know him better. I pray also that the eyes of your heart may be enlightened in order that you may know the hope to which He has called you, the riches of his glorious inheritance in the saints, and his incomparably great power for us who believe..." (Eph 1:17-19).

A personal message: Who am I to write a little handbook for men? My experience with guys in many ways has been awkward and filled with problems. In truth I have been afraid of men for many years, and shut off from them except superficially for most of my life. The good news is that I have been going through some deep healing, and my heart is beginning to open to men, maybe for the first time since early childhood. Love and compassion are pouring through my heart for the pain and struggles you go through. As you walk the Miracle Man journey I will be praying for you. Will you pray for me also?

As you begin: Why don't you ask the Lord to be with you: "Lord Jesus, please help me as I read this book. Open my eyes to the truth You are revealing. Open my ears to hear You speaking. Open my heart to receive Your love. Thank You, Lord. Amen."

Miracles: How many times have you wanted a miracle? Who doesn't need one or many? The dictionary defines a miracle as 'An extraordinary event manifesting divine intervention in human affairs.' God is in the miracle business. We go to Him. Have you seen extraordinary events? Do you want to? The Bible reminds us that miracles come from God: *"You are the God who performs miracles; You display Your power among the peoples"* (Ps 77:14). Are you ready for Him to display His power in you and through you? The Author of Miracles, Jesus Christ, will guide you in this amazing adventure. In His power you can display God's power. As His ambassador you can experience extraordinary events manifesting divine intervention in human affairs. If you want to be God's man of power stand up now, raise your hands and say *"**Yes! I want to be Your Miracle Man!**"*

Know yourself: In your fantasies, how do you want to be known? Do you want people to see you as calm, cool and collected? Or Superman, James Bond, Indiana Jones? A hero in Star Wars or Lord of the Rings? Or perhaps a handsome hero out to rescue a beautiful woman from a dangerous villain? (All the while secretly identifying with someone foolish and vulnerable, like maybe Tim Allen.) The popularity of contact sports, mountain climbing, race car driving, sky diving, anything dangerous, the scarier the better, reveals the need in the heart of men for risk, challenge, competition or daring adventure. Some researchers say it's written into the male DNA. (Or on your hard drive?) Knowing yourself and knowing God are the big issues of life. Lack of knowledge can get you in serious trouble. **Take time to find out who you are and who**

God is. This is adventure to the max. It's the most practical move you can make in your life; and it will save your life. Your unique nature is valuable to God. He wants you to love the man He created. You may look at your emotional nature, your mind, intellect, lack of achievements, and feel disheartened. You may think about the things you have done, mistakes made, sins committed, and want to give up. You may think about things others have done to harm you, even a long list of hurts and rejections, and feel bitterness and rage in your heart. Damaging negative emotions may be holding you prisoner and shutting down your heart. God has help for you. Don't give up.

A message from Budapest: When I was working in Hungary some years ago I asked my translator, Atilla, what he would like me to pray for. His response has touched hearts around the world: *"I want God to wake up my heart!"* Is that what you want, too? Tell Him so: **"God I want You to wake up my heart!"** Now thank Him for what He is about to do. Big changes are on the way.

Meet the One who will wake up your heart: Often people are more open to meet Him when in trouble than in happy times. Desperation can create an opening for God and bring miracles. When I was deeply grieving over the death of my stepson, Randy, I turned on the TV and heard a Christian evangelist inviting listeners to surrender themselves to the Author of Miracles, Jesus Christ. My sad ears tuned in. I was a Christian with knowledge of Jesus but I didn't feel closely connected. When I talked with God that day in front of the TV a real connection was made—up close and personal. I asked Him to come into my heart and He came. Honestly, it was that simple.

Come: He was just waiting for my invitation. He knew I needed to acknowledge Him as my Savior, and commit to Him as Lord. As Savior, He delivers us from the power and effects of sin. To call Him Lord, we acknowledge His divinity and choose Him to be our Master, with authority over us. He is Boss, the One who directs and supervises our lives. He wants so much more for us than we want for ourselves. We don't need to be concerned about the word 'Boss,' but can rejoice that someone cares. He is someone to watch over us, with the capacity to accomplish everything necessary for our lives.

Heart to heart talk: My prayer that day was a simple heart to heart talk with God, opening the door to miracles. It was truly an extraordinary event manifesting divine intervention in human affairs. That was the beginning of my Miracle Woman journey. And it can be the beginning of your Miracle Man journey. Are you thirsty for this? God says, *"Come, all you who are thirsty, come to the waters..."* (Isa 55:1). He says, *"Here I am! I stand at the door and knock. If anyone hears my voice and opens the door, I will come in ..."* (Rev 3:20).

Big trouble and clueless: From what I can see, and what I have heard, men are in really big trouble everywhere. They are mixed up, restless, frustrated, depressed and out of control. Many have been deeply hurt, by parents, marriage partners, friends, others. They have been sinned against and don't know how

4

to respond or be healed. Does any of the following describe how you feel inside: Confused, lonely, withdrawn, desperate, hopeless, disillusioned, hurt, sad, angry, afraid, ashamed, cynical, alone, abandoned, betrayed, vulnerable, left behind, just barely hanging on, scrounging out an existence? Many feel enormous pressures financially, at home and at work. Others are suicidal, or into gambling, sexual extremes, addictions, drugs, violence and abuse of power. Still more feel dead, dull, lost, hollow and empty, with no purpose in life. Fearing failure they have given up. They are filled with regrets, their hearts are broken. Many are unfaithful—to their spouses, friends, themselves and God. Self-deception is rampant. Men everywhere are grieving in ways they don't even understand. They are on the wrong track, crying out internally, "I have become what I don't want to be!" They have compromised to get ahead. Feeling like a failure, they are clueless about where to go for help. They don't know who they are, or why they are here. They have lost their sense of humor. They are without mission and purpose. 'Is this all there is?' is a secret cry. Some go to drugs and alcohol or associate with those who do the same. They find ways to rationalize the behavior even though deep down they know it is wrong. Many feel misunderstood, rejected and are afraid to trust anyone. Some don't even allow themselves to feel. Is that you?

Help! Perhaps you identify with this scripture: *"Save me, O God, for the waters have come up to my neck. I sink in the miry depths, where there is no foothold. I have come into the deep waters; the floods engulf me. I am worn out calling for help..."* (Ps 69:1-3). My friend, hang on. Help is on the way. *"...in all these things we are more than conquerors through him who loved us"* (Ro 8:37).

The bottom line: God is love. That's the bottom line. The world has messed up the word 'love,' but all of our hearts are hungry for the true love that only God can give. A heart connected with Him is open and alive. As the connection deepens, there is an awareness of rightness, a sense of dignity and purpose. You begin to feel worthwhile, valuable. Coming to know Him you discover that His goal is to help you become the fully alive man He created you to be. He will help you with priorities and tough choices. He will guide you on an amazing adventure, teach you what you need to learn, empower and protect you. He tells you: *"For I know the plans I have for you, declares the Lord, plans to prosper you and not harm you, plans to give you hope and a future"* (Jer 29:11). Men, please hear me. **God really does love you.** Let me help you break down any resistance and doubt. You can connect with Him to get your life on track and restore you to your true manhood as His Miracle Man. Let yourself be challenged, to be stimulated to action. "Men need to be challenged to the hilt," says my friend Rod. "They need to know that loving Jesus isn't just words, but it is a matter of life and death." Stop and think for a moment, how does that make you feel? Encouraged? Scared? Hopeful?

Tech support: So where do you go for help? Now is the time to face the truth and decide where you are going for help. Be careful, because your life is valuable to God. (I wanted to say 'precious,' but a male reader said that isn't a guy word!) Some make good, but worldly attempts to deal with things. Secular counselors can help uncover and deal with certain things but may not understand the grace, power and true freedom that spiritual healing does release. Others get seriously off track when they go to healers who use power that is not from Jesus Christ. This can sometimes mask what really needs to be healed and bring in much more serious problems that even block true healing. God is wonderfully possessive of those who belong to Him. My mother got off track and dabbled in psychic forces in her twenties, until the Lord pulled her up short, saying, "Elizabeth, that's enough. Come out of there." She had given her heart to Jesus in college, then in a time of temptation, explored other sources of power (psychic healers, fortune tellers, etc.). She was temporarily trapped in the fascination of a forbidden area. *But when God tells us to do something, He gives us the grace to do it.* She listened to the Lord, repented and turned away. She was forgiven and restored. (Those who get really deep in the psychic realm or new age might require help to get extricated. But remember, **nothing** is impossible with God.) He may be saying to you right now, "Come out of there." If that applies to you, tell Him: "Lord, I want to be all Yours. Remove from me whatever is not Your best, even if I don't understand." How does this make you feel? Free? Cared for? Worried? God has really good plans for you. Keep reading.

God's love letter: The Holy Bible is God's love letter to the world—to you. It's the Manufacturer's Handbook in which you find directions for becoming all He created you to be. It provides wisdom, knowledge and understanding about the essentials of life. It tells all about salvation, healing, restoration and growth. It provides practical guidance for life and relationships, character issues, moral conduct, healthy boundaries, and more. A Miracle Man needs a Bible to know who he is and how to live the life he has been given.

In the beginning there was God. He is One—Father, Son and Holy Spirit. Everything flows out of His love because He *is* Love. God the Son, Jesus, was a man in every way, experiencing all that man experiences except sin. As Savior, He understands and rescues us from all that hinders. *"The thief comes only to steal and kill and destroy; I have come that they may have life; and have it to the full"* (Jn 10:10). The Father and Son empower you with the Holy Spirit. He provides daily help in practical ways. The Holy Spirit is your teacher, counselor, guide, healer, friend and more. He is the loving power guiding our days, pointing the way to light and truth, and warning when we stray. *"Who shall separate us from the love of Christ? Shall trouble or hardship or persecution…?…No, in all these things we are more than conquerors through him who loved us. For I am convinced that neither death nor life… nor anything else in all creation, will be able to separate us from the love of God that is in Christ Jesus our Lord"* (Ro 8:35-39). How does that make you feel? Happy? Peaceful? Loved?

The issue of feelings: Guys often have trouble with this. Why focus on feelings? Well, recognizing feelings helps get in touch with the voice of your heart, which helps you awaken to the word and voice of God. And you really need to hear from God. In my book *True Confessions,* which is about deep healing, I help readers get in touch with hidden feelings and difficult issues. If you have been in the military you have probably been toughened to drive emotions underground—maybe for survival. Or perhaps you were trained at home to tough it out. 'Big boys don't cry,' etc. Feelings are God-given powerful forces to help us. If they are buried they don't stay buried, but rise to the surface in ways that may be harmful. We need to acknowledge feelings while not being governed by them. Sometimes ask, 'What am I feeling right now?' Ask the Lord for help with data retrieval, to connect you with feelings that have been locked in a storage facility. Then listen to what comes up. Talk to a godly friend about what you are feeling. Knowing yourself is critical to your welfare.

Jim's reflections on feelings: "It's very difficult for men to get in touch with their feelings," said a friend, Jim, after reading a first draft of this book, "let alone express them in relationships or to God." He continued, "I like the idea of men exploring their feelings through the act of prayer. It can initially be awkward, but must be cultivated to form a deeper relationship. For me personally, this was found in the scriptures. I could see God's relationship with man through adversity and joy. Through understanding God's nature and how He wanted us to act, we would know what pleased Him. Little did we know that by pleasing Him, we would be blessed with His bounty and peace. That particular understanding and trust is misunderstood greatly today."

Rise up: The world needs leaders, those who will fight for worthy causes. God says "Follow Me and I will make you a leader" (Mk 1:17 paraphrase). He needs

His people in positions of leadership in homes, schools, cities, governments and throughout the world. He needs both men and women filled with His power who are willing to put blood, sweat and tears into the battle to fight for His people and His purpose. He needs those willing to do their part to live out what He has meant for them to be. He may be saying to you, "Come, be someone to be reckoned with." He could even be telling you, "In Me you have what it takes to fight the battle, to live the adventure, to rescue My people and further My plan." Once when I was enroute to Asia to speak at a conference I was frightened and wanted to go home. God spoke to my heart as I flew over the Pacific, ***"Rise up into who you are and fill the position I have given you!"*** Perhaps He is saying to you now, "Rise up and take your place. Fill the position I have prepared for you." Once He said to me, "I will take you as far as you want to go. You set the limits." That message is for you, too. If you say, "This far and no more," He will still love you forever. But how much better if you make this choice: "All the way with You, Jesus." *"... we are God's workmanship, created in Christ Jesus to do good works, which God prepared in advance for us to do"* (Eph 2:10). How does that make you feel? Eager? Encouraged? Empowered?

More from Jim: "Rising up is an important concept for me. Men are driven differently than women. They fear falling short or looking weak. **Today, men are missing in action.** They need to take their place to right many of the breakdowns in our families and society. God's Miracle Men need to rise up and reclaim their position. This will re-establish their relationship with the Lord and give them renewed purpose in life."

Now Choose Life: No one can live your life for you. You may come from terrible circumstances and feel justified in blaming those who raised you, and those who hurt you along the way. You don't have to stay stuck there. Let God Himself make up the difference between what you needed and what you received. He is the only one who can, and He is willing. **Turn from your focus on the past, live in the present, face your future, accept the current condition of your life and grow from it.** Some call it 'owning your pain.' You have a personal responsibility and a real opportunity to choose for yourself the plan of God! You may have a lot of growing to do, but so what? We all have to start somewhere. Now is a good time. Because of hurts and wrong choices you may have shut down at an earlier stage. Maybe you are still a teenager emotionally. No matter. Start where you are now. God tells you, *"...I have set before you life and death... **Now** choose life, so that you and your children may live, and that you may love the Lord your God, listen to his voice, and hold fast to him. **For the Lord is your life...** "* (Dt 30:19-20). Choosing life is your best option! All through life you have choices to make that affect your destiny. When you recognize wrong choices and bring them to Jesus in humble repentance, He will bring His good through it all. *"...in all things God works for the good of those who love him..."* (Ro 8:28). The good news is that the choices you have made, good and bad, have brought you to this important moment of considering fresh options. Now is the time to let go of the old and face tomorrow with Jesus. **Right now, make a decision for Him and the course of your life will flow from that choice.** Are you ready? (Just say yes!)

He knows your potential: God is your loving Father. His love is reflected in the gift of His Son. He continually pours His love into you through the Holy Spirit (Ro 5:5). You may identify with the prodigal son in Luke 15 who took his inheritance and left home, lost it all and was miserable and alone. But guess what? Wherever you are, whatever you have done, the Father will welcome you just as you are. He doesn't tell you to get cleaned up first, then come. You may see yourself as a big slobby mess, and still He says come as you are. (He knows your potential!) The word 'Come' is big with Jesus. He will come to meet you, embrace you and put His mantle of love around you. Hey, the cape Miracle Man is wearing on the book cover is not really a Superman cape, but something much better. **It is God's mantle of love and power!** Filling you with His wonderful presence, He will listen to you, understand you, forgive you....and throw a party for your safe return. He says, "Welcome home, My son." You may have done your best with the resources available to you in the past, or maybe you didn't. He loves you either way. He provides loving care for your soul, strength to accept the present and courage to embrace the future. (Sometimes that help may come through trained Christian counselors or even a wise prayer partner who will work with you to release barriers of the past.) So, why wait? Be present to the gift of this special moment. Stop and listen. He is touching you even now. Be careful not to lose the wonder and the power of this moment.

Online with Jesus: You are invited to enter a Miracle Man Week, with daily prayers (conversation with God) and tips to help you learn to walk in His power. These

few minutes a day will help you map out and expı
a new path for your life, one day at a time. I challenge
you to try it for a week, then a month, then another
month, and another, and see what happens. You have
nothing to lose and everything to gain. You can also
pray the *"Miracle Man Minute"* for a regular tune-up.
"The Lord your God is with you, he is mighty to save.
He will take great delight in you, he will quiet you with
his love, he will rejoice over you with singing" (Zep
3:17).

Starter Prayer
This is a starter prayer to prime the pump, not a
formula. God is personal and will help you find your
own words.

Dear Lord, here I am. This is my starting point with
You. I have a hard time expressing myself, so please
look inside for the unspoken thoughts. Thank You for
giving me a plan of action and tools for the journey.
I need to talk to You (pray) about some issues and
direction for my life. Thank You for opening my ears
to hear You. I want to recognize Your voice, understand
and obey Your guidance. Remind me to check in with
You regularly.* Help me to believe this is possible. I
want to be Your Miracle Man, even though I don't yet
understand what this means. I trust You to teach me.
Thank You for all You are doing in my life…(Continue
in your own words.) In Jesus' Name I pray. Amen.

(*One way to check in, is to frequently ask: "Lord,
what should I do about this situation?" or "How should
I respond to that circumstance?" Then quietly be alert
for what comes next. It will settle gently into your
spirit as an inner awareness.)

cle Man Day One — The dventure of Surrender

..... nfess with your mouth, Jesus is Lord, and believe in your heart that God raised him from the dead, you will be saved" (Ro 10:9).

> **Word List:**
> Christian: Belonging to Jesus Christ
> Adventure: An exciting or remarkable experience
> Surrender: To give yourself over to Jesus Christ, your Savior; to let Him be your Lord
> Receive: To take; to act as a container for; to permit to enter
> Prayer: An earnest request to God in word or thought, also a conversation with God
> Practical: Useful in bringing about good; effective in producing results
> Restore: Renew; to make new; rebuild, revive

A Message from God in Africa: When I was in an African nation on a ministry trip I was overwhelmed by the needs of God's people. After speaking to 5,000 people, I cried to God, "The needs are so great and I am so little!" His response stole my heart: ***"Little in My hands is much."*** "Oh God," I wailed, "help me get into Your hands." Being little in His hands is the beginning of becoming a Miracle Man. It's a practical solution to life circumstances. What may seem like weakness is in fact true strength. *"...my power is made perfect in weakness"* (2Co 12:9).

And then in Trinidad: In a gathering of 800 people on this Caribbean island I challenged people to stand up (take a stand) and declare that they belonged to Jesus. I describe it as 'stepping over the line,' saying, "Jesus,

14

knowing who You are, I give my life to You." The next morning a person told me, "When I stepped over the line last night, God healed my back." Wow! The Lord was teaching us something important about the practical healing effects of surrendering to Him.

More from Rod (a friend who is walking through the discipline and process of AA): "When I surrendered and admitted that I was an alcoholic, God set me free and gave me renewed strength to carry out His plan." There is something urgent about giving ourselves over to Jesus and letting Him be our boss!

Talk to the Lord something like this: Lord Jesus, thank You for Your love. I want to know and believe in Your love for me. Jesus, I need You. Please come into my heart and wake it up. I'm sorry for everything in my life that is less than Your best. I let go of all that stands in the way of receiving Your life and Your power. I turn from sin and accept You and all You are. I receive You as my Savior and Lord and place myself in Your hands. I believe You are the Son of God who became man. I believe You lived and died and rose again and sent the Holy Spirit to give me new life. I receive that new life. Please fill me with Your Holy Spirit and everything I need to live a good life. I give You permission to heal me, restore me, deliver me, and guide me all the days of my life. Knowing You are God, I give my life to You... (Continue in your own words.) In Jesus' Name I pray. Amen.

Listen to what the Lord might say to you. *"Beloved son, thank you for not letting your head shut off your heart. Peace. I am waking up your heart. I love you.*

Lean your heart toward Me in prayer. With My life flowing through you, heartbeat to heartbeat, you can rise up and be all I created you to be. You are My man, My chosen instrument for many good things. I will be for you what you need Me to be. In My hands you will have everything you need to live a good life. Talk to Me about what's going on in your life. As you surrender control to Me I will be able to work with you in restoring you to My highest purpose. Let Me send people into your life to help you grow and keep you strong." (How does this make you feel? Relieved? Hopeful? Valued?)

Bible verses to wake up your heart. (Reflect on each verse and ask yourself, 'How does this make me feel?' Listen to your heart. Mark the messages that leap off the pages and speak to your heart as a special personal word from the Lord to you. He is forming in you a new heart that is open to Him and His love.)

"...to all who received him, to those who believed in his name, he gave the right to become children of God..." (Jn 1:12).

"For God so loved the world that he gave his one and only Son, that whoever believes in him shall not perish but have eternal life" (Jn 3:16).

"...if anyone is in Christ, he is a new creation; the old has gone, the new has come" (2 Co 5:17).

(See also Tit 3:4-6, Ps 32:10, Eze 36:26, Pr 23:26, Ps 40:8, Ps 143:10, 1Th 5:23, Pr 3:5, 1Co 3:16, Isa 58:11)

Miracle Man Day Two — Rip Roaring Heart Cleansing

"Search me, O God, and know my heart...See if there is any offensive way in me, and lead me in the way everlasting" (Ps 139:23-24).

Word List:

Cleanse: To rid of impurities, as if by washing; free of corruption; characterized by clarity and transparency

Rip roaring: noisily excited; victorious

Repentance*: Concrete recognition of offenses, being genuinely sorry, determination to change, asking for and receiving forgiveness

Obstacle: Something that impedes progress or achievement

Grace: Unmerited divine assistance

(*If Catholic or from another sacramental church, repentance could include confession, or the Sacrament of Reconciliation. This is a very healing experience.)

It happened in Northern Ireland: We were preparing for a day of healing when I missed an appointment arranged by my host. He was very angry. With my nose in the air I proclaimed self-righteously, "It was not all my fault." Then the Holy Spirit told me to let go of my need to be right—to take the rap. **When God asks us to do something, He gives us the grace to do it.** When I asked forgiveness from my host, a huge obstacle was removed. As we came together in prayer, my host told me there would be a ball of fire in my hands at the meeting, and there would be miracles. (He had seen it in an interior vision.) Later, other people reported seeing the ball of fire. Powerful healings were reported. (I like to think the stars in Miracle Man's hands on the book cover are like that ball of fire, representing healing power from heaven!)

Talk to the Lord, something like this: (These are just starter ideas. Pick and choose, using your own words.) Dear Lord, I want a rip roaring heart cleansing time with You. First I want to say that in the past I have justified my behavior because of the hurts people have done to me. No more excuses! I am ashamed of some things I have done. I feel dirty and unclean. I have sinned with gambling, sex, incest, pornography, dirty fantasies. I have been unfaithful, had affairs, been abusive, stolen, been prejudiced. I have been out of control with drugs and alcohol. I have abandoned my responsibilities as a man, as a husband, friend, father and son. I have set a bad example and hurt others. I've been insensitive to their needs. I have not provided for those You entrusted to my care; I have not protected them or kept them safe. I have lacked integrity; I've been deceptive, even with myself. I have lied, staying on the edge of truth so it would be believed. I have gone to psychics and opened myself to occult spirits. I have been suicidal, rebellious, stubborn and gone my own independent way. I have been selfish, self-centered, greedy, bitter, resentful, jealous and judgmental. I have been violent, angry and abusive. I have focused on false external securities of money, prestige and power instead of depending on You. I have lost control and yielded to temptation in many ways. What have I missed? I know there is more…. (Continue in your own words. Be still and listen carefully. He is removing major obstacles and freeing you to grow.)

Repent: Lord, I recognize my sins and offenses. I am

sorry, and I choose to stop behaving this way. Please forgive me. I repent of all these sins and dedicate myself to changing my life and correcting the wrongs. I reject sin and repent of not walking in Your truth. I reject evil in all its forms and refuse to let sin control me any more. I reject Satan and all his works and ways. I renounce false worship and every power apart from God (eg., astrology, fortune telling, magical arts and occult games). Please open my mind to the dangers and cleanse me from all connections to psychic forces. I cut any unholy bonds between me and anyone else... (Continue in your own words.) Thank You, Lord, for cleaning me up. Amen.

Listen to what the Lord might say: *"Son, I forgive you and I pour forth My mercy and grace to help you change. You just haven't learned all I want to teach you. I love you and I am proud of you for coming to Me. I will help you make amends. As you come to Me in truth and humility and let Me wash you clean, I will restore you. You have been hiding because you felt guilty. This can now change. I will help you defeat temptation. As you let Me provide your strength, your impulse control, you will become stronger little by little. I am here to be for you what you need Me to be. I love you."* (Reflect on how this makes you feel: Peaceful? Free? Exhausted?) *"...he died for all, that those who live should no longer live for themselves but for him who died for them..."* (2Co 5:15).

Scriptures to wake up your heart:

"If we confess our sins, he is faithful and just and will forgive us our sins and purify us from all unrighteousness" (1Jn 1:9).

"... put off your old self, which is being corrupted by its deceitful desires; to be made new in the attitude of your minds; and to put on the new self, created to be like God in true righteousness and holiness" (Eph 4:22-24).

"How much more, then, will the blood of Christ, who through the eternal Spirit offered himself unblemished to God, cleanse our consciences from acts that lead to death, so that we may serve the living God" (Heb 9:14).

(See also 2Co 5:17-18, Ps 65:3, 1Jn 1:7, Ps 51:2, 1Co 6:11, 2Co 7:11, Jn 3:17, La 2:19, Eze 36:25)

Miracle Man Day Three — The Excitement of Empowerment

"You did not choose me, but I chose you and appointed you to go and bear fruit—fruit that will last. Then the Father will give you whatever you ask in my name" (Jn 15:16).

Word List:

Empower: To enable and equip

Enable: To provide with the means and/or opportunity

Anointed: To make amazingly possible; divinely appointed

Embrace: To take in; to welcome

Baptism in the Spirit: God's gift to you for a wonderful life

Immersed: Plunged into; absorbed

Freedom: Absence of constraint in choice or action; liberation

Ready: Prepared for immediate experience or action; willingly disposed

Spiritual Language: the gift of edifying prayer from 1Co 12

Blessing: Bring pleasure or contentment to; approval; encouragement

---

Here's my story: Alone in my room, listening to a television evangelist, I surrendered my heart to Jesus and asked for the power of His Holy Spirit to fill my life. Flooded with His love, I was baptized in (immersed in) the Holy Spirit and began to pray in a spiritual language, words I didn't understand but God did. This was wonderful, miracle working communication between myself and God. This was an empowering event that shook me to my roots in a good way. I also knew deep inside that I would never be alone again. Wow! Then the exciting journey (boot camp) began: The awakening, the connection with a faith community, the discipline and process of steady growth, the vision for a more meaningful life, the love of scripture. In Daniel 10:12 we learn he *"...set his mind to gain understanding and humbled himself before the Lord."* Both are important to empowerment. Some describe how God healed their marriage and brought unity into the family. A priest friend, Father Kenny, once said as a marriage counselor his first step was to get couples in trouble to be baptized in the Holy Spirit. Then the Holy Spirit began guiding them into healing for their marriage. Following this empowerment many men move forward productively in their personal lives and ministries. One man was able to start a new career. Another began a men's group. Another began to visit prisons. Others branch out in all kinds of creative and unique ministries and life projects and activities. He does have a plan for you, too. He will show you, step by step.

Talk to the Lord something like this: Lord, I come to You and set my mind to gain understanding and humble myself before You. I am ready for Your personal boot camp. I'm available. Only by Your power, guided by Your Spirit, can my life be fruitful. Holy Spirit, fill me, use me, empower me. I want every purpose You have for my life to be fulfilled. Thank You for cleansing the wounds and scars of the past. Thank You for showing me the truth of who I am in the light of Your love. Only You can give me a true picture of myself, because You are my Creator. I am ready to believe I am loved, forgiven, fully known, understood, accepted, cherished and valuable. I am ready to stand up in the knowledge that I am loveable just as I am. Thank You that I don't have to be perfect to be loved. I come to You in repentance and forgiveness and get on with life. I am ready to accept my feelings and ask to be no longer ruled by them. I am ready to love and forgive, reach out to others in healthy ways, grow and change and explore new possibilities. I am ready to believe that my happiness depends on being Your son, not on circumstances. I am ready to accept the power of Your Holy Spirit in my relationships. I am ready to respond in healthy ways. I am ready to let go of destructive behavior, addictions and temptation. I am ready to let You conquer my bad habits and give me courage to say 'yes' to the good and 'no' to the bad.

I am ready — because I choose to receive the empowerment of Your Spirit and I am staying very close to You, wanting to receive… (Continue in your own words.) *"...where the Spirit of the Lord is there is freedom"* (2Co 3:17). *"I will walk about in freedom, for I have sought out your precepts"* (Ps 119:45).

Listen to what the Lord might say: *"My son, I am blessing you right now as you draw ever closer to Me. I have purchased your freedom. As you depend on Me step by step, I can release amazing things through you. Closeness with Me and empowerment walk hand in hand. There is a battle to fight and I will help you fight it. There is a war to be won and I want you in My army. To maintain and increase your strength, I want you connected to others of Mine who will give you courage and build your faith. I don't want you isolated and alone."* (How does this make you feel? Curious? Willing? Wondering how He will do it?) *"For none of us lives to himself alone and none of us dies to himself alone"* (Ro 14:7).

23

Scripture to wake up your heart:

"May the God of peace...equip you with every good thing for doing his will, and may he work in us what is pleasing to him..." (Heb 13:20-21).

"...you will receive power when the Holy Spirit comes on you; and you will be my witnesses...to the ends of the earth" (Ac 1:8).

"We are therefore Christ's ambassadors, as though God were making his appeal through us..." (2Co 5:20).

(See also Php 4:19, 2Sa 22:40, Isa 41:10, Isa 40:31, Eph 3:16, Ps 91, 2Co 12:9, Zec 4:6, Mic 3:8, Eph 6:10-18, 1Th 5:8)

Miracle Man Day Four — The Challenge of Loving

"May the Lord make your love increase and overflow for each other…" (1Th 3:12).

> **Word List:**
> Love: Unselfish, loyal and benevolent concern for the good of another
> Challenge: A summons that is provocative or stimulating
> Faithful: Loyal, constant, steadfast; resisting temptation to betray
> Protect: To guard, shield from injury, defend

Elizabeth and Charlie: Elizabeth was a college educated Christian and Charlie was an uneducated Dutch atheist. These are my parents. All her life Mom prayed, "Lord teach me to love. I don't know how to love. Teach me." She was plagued with Dad's unfaithfulness, with his running away to Mexico with another woman, with his lack of spirituality. She struggled with the educational barrier and his disabilities (half blind and almost deaf, and more). Still, the Lord held her in place, praying for him and loving him when she didn't always feel like it. She read 1Co 13 over and over: *"Love is patient, love is kind. It does not envy, it does not boast, it is not proud. It is not rude, it is not self-seeking, it is not easily angered, it keeps no record of wrongs…It always protects, always trusts, always hopes, always perseveres. Love never fails…"(*1Co 13:4-8). She read it until it became a part of her and she could say, "God's love **in me** is patient… kind...etc." Dad was on his deathbed when the Lord woke up his heart to cry out for Him. Accepting Jesus, he was physically healed of the effects of a paralyzing stroke and lived another five years. All the years of Mom's 'other centered' sacrifice of love broke through the generations of resistant atheism in his family line. After Mom died I read in her prayer journal, "Thank You Lord for teaching me how to live Your love. I'm so glad You didn't let me off the hook with Charlie."

Living His love: Their story has touched countless lives, reminding us that **God's love is a breakthrough force.** It reinforces our understanding that love is a sacrifice; it is not about getting our own way. Living God's love is a whole new dimension of life, and probably what He will gently review with us when we arrive in heaven. He challenges us to hold onto the importance of loving in all life's relationships, and reminds us that He will provide all the help we need (Php 4:19). The world tells us the lie that love is having someone else meet our needs and when that fails we stop loving. God's love raises us above what the world teaches.

Talk to the Lord, something like this: Dear Lord, please teach me to live Your love. I have looked for love in all the wrong places instead of looking for ways to share Your love. I've been afraid to love, afraid to trust, afraid I'll be hurt again. Holding myself at a distance, I isolated my heart and locked out love. Please forgive me. Your nature is love; I want to know and feel that love, and share it with others. Teach me how to be a loving person, husband, father, son, friend… (Continue in your own words.) Thank You, Lord. Amen.

Listen to what the Lord might say: *"Beloved, I will teach you to love and help you heal and grow. I know your tender side and your tough side, the sensitive and the rock hard. My love can penetrate every sorrow, every fear, every stony barrier. Come to Me now. Receive My compassionate word in Psalm 139: "I have searched you and I know you…I am familiar with all your ways…I created your inmost being; I knit you together in your mother's womb and you are fearfully and wonderfully made…I know your heart and I will lead you in the way everlasting." My son, the enemy of your soul has lied to you, and told you not to love. When you were hurt he prompted you to make vows to lock up your heart. Give Me permission to go deep inside and speak truth into your soul. Even now I impart My true love into the lies of unlove deep in your heart. Receive now, My son. My love is for you, always."* (How does this make you feel? Valuable? Empowered? Loveable?)

Scriptures to wake up your heart:

"…hope does not disappoint us, because God has poured out his love into our hearts by the Holy Spirit, whom he has given us" (Ro 5:5).

"…the fruit of the Spirit is love, joy, peace, patience, kindness, goodness, faithfulness, gentleness and self control" (Gal 5:22-23).

"…we know and rely on the love God has for us. God is love. Whoever lives in love lives in God, and God in him" (1Jn 4:16).

(See also 1Jn 3:16, 1Jn 4:10, 1Th 4:9, Heb 3:13, Jude 21, Eph 5:2, 1Pe 4:8, 1Co 2:9, 1Jn 3:1, Isa 49:16, Jer 31:3, Ro 5:5, Eph 2:4-5, 2Th 3:5, 1Co 13)

Miracle Man Day Five — The Force of Forgiveness

"Get rid of all bitterness, rage and anger, brawling and slander, along with every form of malice. Be kind and compassionate to one another, forgiving each other, just as in Christ God forgave you" (Eph 4:31-32).

Word List:

Force: To hasten the rate of progress or growth; overcoming resistance

Forgiveness: To give up resentment and bitterness; to pardon; to cancel a debt

Kindness: Sympathetic, helpful, compassionate

Grieve: To feel a deep and poignant distress caused by a loss; sorrow

Let: To permit; to give opportunity to

Repent: To change our mind; to turn a different way

More about Dad: But first, let me say before I forget: ***Repent, forgive and watch the Spirit move!*** When I was young Dad touched me in sexual ways. I shut down my heart and locked the door. My relationships with men were superficial and cold, manifesting in divorce and unhealthy interactions. For years I prayed for healing with Dad. In his final hours when he was in a coma, I sat at his side and called out to God for healing. A holy presence came into the room, and Dad spoke to me in the silence, spirit to spirit, "I'm sorry!" The words reached back to the wounded little girl, Linda, and something healed and opened up inside. I said gently, "I forgive you, Daddy." The next day Jesus took him home. Because of that time I was able to let go, grieve the loss and become willing to love. And the Spirit has been able to move through me in many new ways.

Release to God's mercy: Forgiveness is central to the heart of Jesus. When someone does you wrong, Jesus can help you move from hurt to healing if you let Him. **Letting** is key. Open your heart and **let** Him. At some point in our lives we need to release the past to God's mercy, place the future in His hands, and simply live in the present. *Now* is God's special gift to us. (Some say that's why it's called the present!)

Talk to the Lord, something like this: Lord, I want Your truth. Wake up my heart to Your miracle of forgiveness. Give my heart so much of Your love that resistance is overcome and something deep inside is released. If there is a family pattern of unforgiveness, grudges or prejudice, please uproot it now. I don't want it. Please give me the grace to accept the fullness of Your love and extend that love generously. Bring to mind a person I need to forgive. I now choose to forgive that person because I want to be open to You. I take responsibility for my feelings about others' actions and make a decision to forgive and let go of the hurt. Bless them better than if they were nice to me. I am willing to take steps toward reconciliation as You lead me. And Lord, I make a covenant of forgiveness with You. I choose to keep my heart open to forgiving others and even forgiving myself as You have forgiven me. I am not going to live in unforgiveness anymore… (Continue in your own words.) In Jesus' Name. Amen.

Listen to what the Lord might say: *"My Miracle Man, My son, **forgiveness is another breakthrough force.** As you look to Me, I will give you all the help you need to be a man of forgiveness. Miracles large* and small will flow in your life and relationships as you walk this narrow path of power. Climb up into the high country with Me where the air is fresh and clear. **Repent, forgive, and watch My Spirit move.** It is not easy, but then I did not give you My Holy Spirit to do easy things. I love empowering you." (How does that make you feel? Courageous? Hopeful? Strengthened?)

Scriptures to wake up your heart:

"...Father, forgive them, for they do not know what they are doing" (Lk 23:34).

"In him we have redemption through his blood, the forgiveness of sins, in accordance with the riches of God's grace that he lavished on us with all wisdom and understanding" (Eph 1:7-8).

"Bear with each other and forgive whatever grievances you may have against one another. Forgive as the Lord forgave you. And over all these virtues, put on love..." (Col 3:13-14).

(See also Mk 11:25, Ps 103:1-3, Ac 13:38, 1Jn 1:9, Lk 17:4, Eph 4:32, Eph 4:26-27)

Miracle Man Day Six — The Gift of a Grateful Heart

"...let us be thankful, and so worship God..." (Heb 12:28).

Word List:
Gift: Special favor by God; present; something voluntarily transferred by one person to other without compensation
Gratitude: Appreciating, valuing benefits received
Reverence: Extravagant devotion
Practice: To do something repeatedly to become good at it

Jim is forever grateful: "I had been having a bad week, work had its problems and I was tired. At the time we had three small boys which can be a little distracting, and my wife, Mel, and I had just begun attending Mass after a lapse. I was struggling to understand my relationship with the Lord. As I stood in Mass to pray the Lord offered a clarity of His love like I had never known. He told me that He loved me the way I was, and that I could be made perfect in Him because He had blessed our marriage, family and relationships. At first I felt unworthy because of my lack of participation in our relationship. Then my eyes saw all the goodness with which He had blessed my life. Mel looked even more beautiful, my children were God's miracles and blessings through eyes I had not seen. All the little bumps in the road seemed insignificant. That moment was so perfect and such a gift that it will never leave me. For that I am forever grateful. It is a way of seeing God's love fulfilled." *"Thanks be to God for his indescribable gift"* (2Co 9:15).

Talk to the Lord something like this: Lord, please

help me grow in gratitude. Thank You for allowing me to see everything as gift, including the bumps in the road. Thank You for opening Your truth in my mind and revealing Your purpose for my life. Thank You for setting me free from self-centeredness and opening my heart to the needs of others. Thank You for community, family, a place to belong. Thank You for helping me to entrust my life to You in deeper ways. I am grateful for my history that led me to You. Thank You for Your mighty power within, doing exceedingly more than all we can ask or imagine (see Eph 3:20). To You be the glory forever and ever... (Continue in your own words.) Amen.

Listen to what the Lord might say: *"Son, practice being grateful. A grateful heart can take you through moments of pain and sorrow into a deeper relationship with Me. Gratitude releases faith and opens your heart to belief and trust in Me. Be thankful for the things I have sorted out in your life, and also for the things still in process. They will work out for your good and My glory as you continue to place your trust in Me."* (How does this make you feel? Peaceful? Confident? Grateful?)

Scriptures to wake up your heart: (During this time try praying in silence to listen to what God might say. Set a few minutes apart and write what you are thinking at the moment.)

"Do not be anxious about anything, but in everything, by prayer and petition, with thanksgiving, present your requests to God" (Php 4:6).

"...thanks be to God, who always leads us in triumphal procession in Christ..." (2Co 2:14).

"...give thanks in all circumstances, for this is God's will for you in Christ Jesus" (1Th 5:18).

(See also 2Co 3:18, Col 1:12, Col 3:15, 1Pe 2:9, Ps 100:4, Ps 107:22).

Miracle Man Day Seven —The Power of Purpose

"The Spirit of the Sovereign Lord is on me, because the Lord has anointed me to preach good news to the poor. He has sent me to bind up the brokenhearted, to proclaim freedom for the captives and release from darkness for the prisoners…" (Isa 61:1).

Word List:
Purpose: The reason why; guiding principle; aim in view; plan
Interior purpose: worship and reverence; loving God back
Exterior purpose: To build the kingdom of God
Power: The ability to act or produce an effect
Testimony: To tell others the reason for your empowerment so they will see and believe

---

Something God the Father said to me: In the period following my conversion I was filled with the desire to do something meaningful and self-supporting. I didn't want to live for myself alone. Mt. 6:33 became an important scripture: *"…seek first the kingdom of God…"* One morning I heard God the Father say, ***"I will give this to you if you will use the freedom it gives you to honor Me."*** I knew 'this' referred to something meaningful and self-supporting. Many years have passed, and I am living in that reality. Yet there is still something more. Whatever the 'more' is, it will be reason to serve the Lord in an ever deepening relationship; to give to Him extravagantly in response to His amazing gift. That is called worship. Wherever you are, there is always more. His training for your work in the world will be tailored to your uniqueness and talents, and the wonders God has prepared for you. *"The Lord will fulfill his purpose for me…"* (Ps 138:8).

35

Just remember, God's plan for you is to love Him back in all you do; to make Him the whole purpose in life. It won't always be comfortable and easy, as the next story reveals.

He was first sold into slavery: From what I have seen in my travels and in my own life, much of the growth comes through trust when out of a comfort zone. We don't tend to grow when things are wonderful. Forward movement comes as we surrender to the Lord in the midst of trials. (Out on a limb is where the fruit grows!) We can also learn more about growth through trials from examples of Christians who have gone before us. When the Catholic man Vincent de Paul was taken captive by pirates around the year 1600 and sold into slavery he had to submit to humiliation and degradation. During that miserable time as a prisoner he was changed, deepened, softened. God gave him a heart for the poor and needy and formed him for future work that would impact the world. (The St. Vincent de Paul thrift shops and other ministries to the poor are still well known today.) You too have an opportunity to be formed for God's purpose through your own painful struggles. As we are being formed for service in the world, we are also being formed for the inner work of worship. In fact we could say, worship of God becomes service to the world. Worship is not just confined to church. We can worship Him in all that we do. Some people even wash windows for Jesus. *"God is spirit, and his worshipers must worship in spirit and in truth"* (Jn 4:24).

Talk to the Lord, something like this: Lord Jesus, please help me to comprehend your purpose in my life. Take me through the necessary trials and growth experiences to reach Your highest goal for my life. Please change, deepen, soften and strengthen me too. Let me see the trials as a sports training camp. I want to be ready to hit a home run for You, Jesus. I want my life to be a part of something bigger than myself. Show me some needs in the world where You would like me to be involved. Above all, form me in my main interior purpose—to fall in love with You, and worship You with all my heart. I want to know You, love You and serve You all the days of my life… (Continue in your own words.) In Jesus' name I pray. Amen.

Listen to what the Lord might say: *"My Miracle Man, press on with Me. Spend quality time with Me so I will remain in first place with you. Listen to My voice in your heart like a close friend. I want personal fellowship with you. Look forward to your special time with Me and staying in conversation with Me throughout the day, both talking and listening. Keep your attention on Me and remain available in My hands. I want you always to be ready to give others the reason for your empowerment so they too will see and believe. As you keep your focus straight and pure, I will guide you into the most exciting and wonderful adventures of your life."*

Scriptures to wake up your heart:

"Delight yourself in the Lord and he will give you the desires of your heart. Commit your way to the Lord; trust in him and he will do this…" (Ps 37:4-5).

"…I was hungry and you gave me something to eat, I

*was thirsty and you gave me something to drink, I was
a stranger and you invited me in, I needed clothes and
you clothed me, I was sick and you looked after me, I
was in prison and you came to visit me…whatever you
did for one of the least of these brothers of mine, you
did for me"* (Mt 25:35-36, 40).

*"…I heard the voice of the Lord saying, 'Whom shall I
send? And who will go for us?' And I said, 'Here I am,
send me'"* (Isa 6:8).

(See also Ps 29:2, Ps 20:4, Ps 37:23-24, Ps 77:14, 2Pe
3:18, Da 12:3, 1Co 3:8, 2Co 9:6, 1Ti 6:12, Eph 1:11,
Php 3:10, Eph 2:10, Ps 90:17, Da 11:32, Jer 1:1, Col
1:9, Ps 90:17)

Other Things

Learning more: As we set our minds to gain understanding and humble ourselves before the Lord (Da 10:12), the *Catechism of the Catholic Church* is an excellent educational resource. Here are a few quotes: "Faith is first of all a personal adherence of man to God. At the same time, and inseparably, it is a free assent to the whole truth that God has revealed. As personal adherence to God and assent to his truth, Christian faith differs from our faith in any human person. It is right and just to entrust oneself wholly to God and to believe absolutely what he says. For a Christian, believing in God cannot be separated from believing in the One he sent, his 'beloved Son' ...One cannot believe in Jesus Christ without sharing in his spirit. It is the Holy Spirit who reveals to men who Jesus is..." (Catechism 150, 151). "Believing is possible only by grace and the interior helps of the Holy Spirit. But it is no less true that believing is an authentically human act. Trusting in God and cleaving to the truths he has revealed are contrary neither to human freedom nor to human reason. Even in human relations it is not contrary to our dignity to believe what other persons tell us about themselves and their intentions or to trust their promises..."(154). "Believing in Jesus Christ and in the One who sent him for our salvation is necessary for obtaining that salvation..."(161). "The Word of God, which is the power of God for salvation to everyone who has faith, is set forth and displays its power in a most wonderful way in the writings of the New Testament which hand on the ultimate truth of God's Revelation. Their central object is Jesus Christ, God's incarnate Son: his acts, teachings, Passion and glorification, and his Church's beginnings under the Spirit's guidance" (124). (*Catechism of the Catholic Church* ISBNO-89942-256-X. Catholic Book Publishing Company, 257 West 17th St., New York, NY 10011.)

Miracle Man Minute

Lord Jesus, thank You for showing me the way to go, and helping me to live a good life. I know I am not alone. You are home to me. You are Love, and You love me without condition. In coming to know You I come to know myself. Thank You for wanting me, receiving me, washing me and enabling me to come to You. Thank You for loving me until I overflow with love. Thank You for forgiving me so I can be a force for good wherever I am. Thank You for the grace to be thankful and to be a Miracle Man for Your glory… (Add your own words.) Amen.

Inner Healing Prayer based on Psalm 23

THE LORD IS YOUR SHEPHERD, YOU SHALL NOT WANT: Jesus the Good Shepherd and visible sign of the Father gave His life for you in loving obedience to His Father. Your response to that love gives you the right to call God your Father. May you come to know the wonderful Fatherhood of God. May the Holy Spirit deep inside draw you close to your Father. He is your resource in every challenge and provision for every need. May you always remember that you belong to Him and that it's His job and His joy to take care of you.

HE MAKES YOU TO LIE DOWN IN GREEN PASTURES AND

LEADS YOU BESIDE QUIET WATERS. HE RESTORES YOUR SOUL: Your Heavenly Father is loving you right now. May you hear His love words in your soul and feel Him rocking you in His arms. May Jesus, the Living Word, help you to see and reverse any hidden vows to never love again; to never trust; to never let anyone get too close. May you know Him as the God of second chances, and third, and fourth. May you experience deep connection with your Heavenly Father.

HE LEADS YOU IN PATHS OF RIGHTEOUSNESS FOR HIS NAME'S SAKE: May His approval and unconditional love give you a sense of rightness deep inside. As His love permeates your whole being, may you experience your feet being planted on Solid Rock. May your heart become sweet and open, fresh and pure, reflecting the beauty of Jesus and the radiance of the Father.

WHEN YOU WALK THROUGH THE VALLEY OF THE SHADOW OF DEATH YOU WILL FEAR NO EVIL, FOR HE IS WITH YOU. HIS ROD AND STAFF WILL COMFORT YOU: May you trust Him as your courage and know Him as your safety. Jesus is your victory. He is Emmanuel, God with us, and He never goes away. May your heart be awakened to the needs of others. May you reach out to them with His love.

HE PREPARES A TABLE FOR YOU IN THE PRESENCE OF YOUR ENEMIES. HE ANOINTS YOUR HEAD WITH OIL. YOUR CUP OVERFLOWS: May you see and remember how His powerful hand has delivered you in the past. He is the Wall of Fire around you, your safe path through every difficulty. May you experience Him as your empowerment, to go where the Father sends you and do what He wants you to do. He pours His life through you extravagantly. May your heart be filled with gratitude.

SURELY GOODNESS AND MERCY WILL FOLLOW YOU ALL THE DAYS OF YOUR LIFE, AND YOU WILL DWELL IN THE HOUSE OF THE LORD FOREVER: May you know that this favor is yours as a child of the King. Jesus, the Name above all Names, son of the King Immortal, now takes you to the Jordan River and opens your ears to hear the covenant words of your Father: "You are My child whom I love; with you I am well pleased." May these words be engraved on your heart and may you forever say, "Jesus, I trust in You." *This is to my Father's glory that you bear much fruit..." (Jn 15:8).* (From *The Healing Power of a Father's Blessing.*)

Precious Power Prayer: Holy Spirit, come. You are precious evidence of God in my life. You unite me to Jesus and enable me to live in Him. I am welcome, I am family, I belong. I am Your temple, I am Yours. Thank You for loving me. Gift of my Father, power for my life, hope for my soul, I welcome You. Oil and Wind, Water of Life, Breath of life, Precious Dove, Fire and Friend, I love You. Precious Power, Voice of God, You speak and I try to listen. I am learning, slowly. When the world presents lies, I see through to You, my Truth. You guide me onto right paths and away from wrong paths, and bring light where there is darkness. You are Loving Kindness, Consolation, Comfort, Courage, Teacher, Guide, Helper in prayer, Healer, Sanctifier. What a wonder you are. Come Holy Spirit, Precious Power, glorify Jesus for all the world to see. (from the book *Precious Power*)

Order Form

All of Linda Schubert's resource materials can be ordered online at www.linda-schubert.com.

To order using the form below, send payment to Linda Schubert, Miracles of the Heart Ministries, P.O. Box 4034, Santa Clara, CA 95056; Fax (408) 734-8661, Phone (408) 734-8663, E-mail linda@linda-schubert.com.

Books

_____	*Precious Power**..	$ 3.00	_____
_____	*True Confessions**.....................................	$ 3.00	_____
_____	*Miracle Hour**	$ 3.00	_____
_____	*Miracle Moments**	$ 3.00	_____
_____	*Rich in Mercy**	$ 3.00	_____
_____	*Miracle Man Handbook**	$ 3.00	_____
_____	*Miracle Woman Handbook**	$ 3.00	_____
_____	*Healing Power of a Father's Blessing*	$ 3.50	_____
_____	*Five Minute Miracles*	$ 4.95	_____
_____	*Transfigurations, Places of Prayer with Prof. R. England*	$20.00	_____

CD's

_____	Miracle Hour Prayers (Pray along with Linda)	$ 8.00	_____
_____	Double CD Teaching and Miracle Hour Prayers	$14.00	_____
_____	Receive the Gift (Linda's song in English and Spanish).................	$8.00	_____

Tape Album

_____	The Gift of Tongues (Two tape album includes workshop and Linda praying an hour in tongues)...	$10.00	_____

(For complete list of tapes go to www.linda-schubert.com)

Total	$	_____
California residents add 8% tax	$	_____
***Shipping	$	_____
TOTAL ENCLOSED	$	_____
U.S. FUNDS		

Visa _____   Mastercard _____

Name on card _____

Expiration date _____

Card # _____

Ship to _____

_____

_____

Phone_____

*For quantity discount of *True Confessions, Miracle Moments, Rich in Mercy, Miracle Hour, Precious Power, Miracle Man Handbook* or *Miracle Woman Handbook,* use the following chart:

1-25 copies	$3.00 each
26-50 copies	2.75 each
51-99 copies	2.25 each
100+ copies	1.75 each

**Bookstores order Five Minute Miracles from Catholic Book Publishing Co., 77 West End Road, Totowa, NJ 07512, Phone (973) 890-2400. For other books, standard trade discount applies.

***For media rate shipping to U.S. locations, refer to chart below:

1 to	5	items add $2.50
6 to	20	items add $3.50
21 to	35	items add $4.50
36 to	50	items add $5.50
51 to	70	items add $6.50
71 to	100	items add $7.50
100+		items add $8.50 per 100

To Canada double the U.S. shipping cost and send payment in U.S. FUNDS. For shipping to other countries, write for cost.

If you want to schedule Linda and her team for a
Miracle Man workshop in your area write, phone or e-mail
Linda Schubert
Miracles of the Heart Ministries
P.O. Box 4034, Santa Clara, CA 95056
linda@linda-schubert.com
www.linda-schubert.com
Phone (408) 734-8663